100 Notes on Violence is a sustained, haunted meditation on the many ways violence touches us. In this polyphonic poem the voices of caregivers, killers, and children commingle and, disturbingly, sometimes overlap. Innocence and guilt are never far apart. "At the pool the boy in cammies reads an encyclopedia of weapons." This book has great moral complexity, gravitas, and courage. —Rae Armantrout, Judge of the 2009 Sawtooth Poetry Prize

"The book about violence must be a book of quotations," according to Julie Carr in *100 Notes on Violence*. "For everyone speaks about violence." Few have spoken or written on the subject with the desperate accuracy and the incendiary beauty of this disturbing, necessary book. Here, the quotations include statistics and news reports as well as the more traditional poetic forms, all to engage finally a light like that of the sun. "It's daily reassurance, daily assault." —Bin Ramke, author of *Earth on Earth*

100 Notes on Violence takes as its energy source language's violence as imprinted onto the words themselves, each syllable but a microcosm of the macro-level harm we daily inflict on and experience from each other. From the word "launched" miscopied as "launced," the violence carrying over and evolving into a hybrid of "lanced" and launched, to a list of purchasable artillery too much now for one to own or desire, Carr lyrically dissects a trained tolerance for terror and reveals how this centuries-old obsession with harm continues to mature in our hands. *100 Notes on Violence* is a book for today like no other. —Phillip Williams, author of *Mutiny*

100 NOTES ON VIOLENCE

Cover art: "Red Hooded Figure" by Andres Serrano

Cover design by Jeffrey Pethybridge
Cover typeface: Avenir

Interior design by Laura Joakimson
Interior typeface: Apollo MT, and Eurostyle

100 Notes on Violence is the winner of the Sawtooth Poetry Prize in 2009, chosen by Rae Armantrout and was first published by Ahsahta Press, Boise State University in 2010

Library of Congress Cataloging-in-Publication Data

Names: Carr, Julie, 1966- author.
Title: 100 notes on violence / Julie Carr.
Other titles: One hundred notes on violence
Description: Oakland, California : Omnidawn Publishing, 2023. | Includes
  bibliographical references. | Summary: "Back in print, Carr's powerful
  poems seek out and face violence and its counterforces. Julie Carr
  obsessively researches instances of intimate terrorism, looking
  everywhere from Walt Whitman and Emily Dickinson to lists of phobias and
  weapon-store catalogs. She searches for what can be learned from the
  statistics, the statements by and about rapists and killers, the
  websites of hate groups, and the capacity for cruelty that lies within
  all of us. 100 Notes on Violence is a diary, a document, and a dream log
  of the violence that grips America and devastates so many. But Carr also
  offers a layered and lyric tribute to violence's counterforces: love,
  commonality, and care. Her unflinching "notes" provoke our minds and
  burrow into our emotions, leading us to confront our fears and our own
  complicity"-- Provided by publisher.

Identifiers: LCCN 2023019351 | ISBN 9781632431097 (trade paperback)
Subjects: LCSH: Violence--United States--Poetry. | BISAC: POETRY / General
  | POETRY / Women Authors | LCGFT: Poetry.
Classification: LCC PS3603.A77425 A614 2023 | DDC 811/.6--dc23/eng/20230524
LC record available at https://lccn.loc.gov/2023019351

.

Published by Omnidawn Publishing, Oakland, California
www.omnidawn.com
10 9 8 7 6 5 4 3 2 1
ISBN: 978-1-63243-109-7

100 NOTES ON VIOLENCE

JULIE CARR

OMNIDAWN PUBLISHING
OAKLAND, CALIFORNIA
2023

"We love you oh life and we get on your nerves"

Apollinaire

"and recoiling not"

Whitman

1.

It won't snow again, it won't—you can take off your shirt, you can lie on the earth

I'm attracted to children. Feet like little suns

      My brother drew a muscle then he drew a gun
      my envy turned me wild and my wild made me run

In my notebook there are mint leaves   bent around my head

Air's hung with glitter, an early erstwhile ear

      when babies in their pretty rage wake crying

Days of rain, I've loved your   English so solo so done

               Vaulty

      wet sky: an infant mouth on mine

Mint leaves in my hair here, something rotting in my eyes

In my notebook no one's losing it
All the women with their paper scraps

          their files, glosses, glasses, lashes, shawls

I make them custards, make them queens

2.

Salt on the land's low parts, you see it when the planes

carry you

into that
nothing that loves you   Salt's

pretty in the light now, prettier than trees

The beautiful
boys and girls with their Velcroed shoes—

and a man takes his key from his pants

scratches his initial into Plexiglas—an A like a house been condemned

He's twenty-four and done for, you know him from the news,
he's got hay in his heart

and did to them what I cannot write, not in this my—

3.

A BEGINNING

A.

You, sweet compass, are about violence, which I can't.

At the pool the boy in cammies reads an encyclopedia of weapons:

> Black Widow Custom AK47 Johnson semi-Auto Colt 1937 Super Match.

> His sister grins through water in her
>> swimming class.

B.

> I've been thinking about what I can't look at: school shootings, can't google
> it, can't write it into the little space to see what comes up. I'd rather see that
> prostitute's ass as she bends over for the suicidal actor on TV.

>> There's a mandala, a chess set,

>> a Viking helmet, a parasol, dog, sugar daddy,

to stuff into the space from where the voice would emerge that says:

Nothing in this

world is going to adhere to me, not one thing will make one bit of

difference

I am a free and unencumbered

hand

4.

Said the Mama, I'm going to sing to you now, with my profile,
                    a song about fevers and towns

        And the baby took the song to bed, wove it tight to make herself
        a walking bridge, a bird cage, a bride

5.

Hit my jaw on the car door, fell facedown and drunk
sick on wine and drunk on butter, mouthing leather

I'm stealing my friends' hands away; I'm tying up their tongues
I'll heed no more threats of death today, no more lungs of rust

                —Kids poked their names
                into dry leaves with a pen

            Kneading bread dough in the kitchen, I
                (guy shoots himsel—)

        shut   the basement   door

It won't freeze my child, not make her cold, she'll sleep unbothered
        she'll wear my clothes: my notebook, my compass, my blood.

6.

Today was exhausting. The furnace exhausted. Ours

a quiet house, a truce

Still to do: bed, more thoughts, the thinking kind: whether to blindfold the children?

See the ocean? It's really absurd. As if anyone wants that kind of depth

My favorite scholar gave me a pen. What did I use if for? Self-effacement

7.

Sun on the windshield animals my car and I come neatly close to rage

Up to it

Looks like someone made me up. I'm driving around with food for children
Roads flat and regular. Wider if we want
I'll listen to anything: Pakistani rap, weather, geoquiz, biology of lies

Food spills when I round a bend

8.

I pushed my face into the air beside the river
I broke that air with my face my face was hard like an
erection and from my face an emission of sound it
shattered that bit of cold air that was hanging there
above the water like an irresponsible bird, not caring
for its own unity, it let me break it let me even more
ruin it my face was not proud of this not not proud
nothing just did it and kept walking that broken cold air
fell behind me soundless because dead

9.

THE HIDDEN

A.

Rugs on the floor hide something. Even if we think we know what.

Consider this cartoon: a woman with a broom lifts the corner of her carpet,
     is shocked to discover a gaping chasm below!

"Not *if* you buy an alarm system, *when* you buy one!" says the threatening note
     from our neighbor.

In our previous neighborhood, a 16-year-old boy, stabbed at 10 on a major road.
Someone set fire to a house on the block—

     they said he had no motive, or none that could be known—

then set the kids' school aflame: vessels rocking in the windy bay.

A secret camera takes a poll. Frail stars spill into the dark.
Frosted pastries wrapped in plastic: sit idle.

B.

Regarding it all, intently along: so, they stockpiled, they harbored.

Take these, my leaves, my falling off leaves: Confederate Knights, Christian
     Patriots: Make the poems of materials, for they are the most spirited, they the
     most busy:

Aryan Defense League; Confederate Hammerskins: Regarding it all, the broken
      leaves underfoot,
    dusting /:

She said what's a line, a line must know something, something I do not know.
I'd write until the music stopped, but what is that music, the music of
      materials?

We the People; Nationalist Movement: Fanged and glittering…

                        over all. (Whitman)

Flaming Sword, White Viking Revolution: their plans undeveloped, to shoot
      black kids, hadn't
    gotten very far, but //:

      the night presumes to hide.

Your permit to carry is 52.50. That's fingerprints, background. Your "temporary
      emergency permit," just 30 (no background).

Wheel the baby in, let the baby sleep, is there someone above me, just over my
      head? Listen to me, night, my girl needs rest, reveal yourself, show your
      face, the face of her mother

                  standing against the sun.

10.

FIRE

Earliest stars, little princes with ponies. Evening snow

       unworries the branches.

I like women in white dresses. The just-married look, breasts tight—

    I said I've used up my bonus points, spent my rewards. I've maxed out my
    cash attack. Can't drop my kids in the rubber breakfast playground and go
    to the Nature Store. Can't click on one-stop. Can't drive by. What's more
    abstract than snow? Especially now. It means nothing. The wind came up
    and drove the ghost back into the oven.

Standing by the window, the whitened street below,
and something lights, *quiet*, the sky.

11.

FIRE 2

Lamp holder, I'm not dangerous. "Let fire" in Wendy's, not
me, that wasn't me, that was my brother, my gorgeous

going nowhere friar. Put his hands in the river and pulled out
      a passage. (River water boiling)

Fat and named dumber he lumbered the grocery aisles like one whose body
      wore him

      out. Oranges, chips, bars, nuts:
      eyed him from their posts.

12.

THE REAL

A.

The war machine resembles an animal yet also a supernatural being …it understands atmosphere: how to suspend reality, how to create the black hole. (Taussig)

And one hopes that by taking notes one can replace "real" experience with "real" text.

I saw a woman smack her child on a Metro platform in Paris
so hard he fell over.

> There grew

a quietness //

The kid, sitting there on the floor, both slack and plump, reminded me of a leather purse in the hand of the 3rd and foolish son who has given all his riches to a hungry hag.

That night I dreamed I had sex with a cat. In the morning as I was buying my coffee, a real cat ran by my ankles. I almost fainted with desire and fear.

B.

Heat sways the hanging lamp
overhead.   Pages ascend toward

daylight—the blue, unpublished, hand of God. (Vallejo)

> Nearby: another child-voice, cleansed: oh—

13.

In my twenties I imagined I might reverse my body
get the organs out—I know you don't believe me, but I
wasn't very kind to—

14.

He's got a knife in the pocket and a phone in the neck, some cash, some wool,
        something wet in the head.

He "let fire" in a Wendy's, and a medic and his family (Jane's Addiction in his bud)—

they "went down."

                Bullet: bowl: blister: to
                lambaste: to thrash: to strike: to

                endure or lift up: or harden, the

hand, broken like gravel, like a riverbank, eroded, and so

free.

15.

There's the useful mother and the useless one
Useless is dead in its radiant face,
endlessly dead, eating and hot

Useful in motion, most lively in its own
erasure

16.

      Annie was a Buddhist and wouldn't kill a bug
      so the bugs killed all the plants when my mother went away

Brenda in the red house
got cancer in her breast

           Her little boy rode a pony

17.

Never been to Texas, never been to Spain, never been to
Holland, never been to Maine

All you babies with your orbs
like planets hung in space

with your mouths around your feet
you crawl into my face

18.

Dear child,

"Maybe now we're beginning to see the long-term consequences of a young life hooked up to a
black rainbow of behavior altering drugs."

Dear child,

A quarry in the woods

Dear child,

simple, simple, easy, easy, quiet, quiet, still

19.

WEST

Date: Fri, 29 Feb 2008 13:58:00 -0700   7 of 1601
From: Steve Nelson <s.nelson@earthlink.net>
Subject: Re: Texas
To: Julia Alice Carr <Julie.Carr@colorado.edu>

The West is so mean, and Texas is the worst. Next comes Colorado. I
come from a very rough place, but you never hurt a GIRL, or a KID, Or
an OLD PERSON. I'm not saying it never happened, but it was shameful.
When I was about 50, I had a girlfriend about 25 (a situation made for
disaster). When her brother bludgeoned both their parents to death while
they were sleeping in their quiet suburban home in xxxx, one with a
bowling pin, one with a golf club, I had to bring her the news. A
friend heard it on the radio. We were just splitting up, I think
because she was having premonitions as to what was going to happen. Her
brother had just gotten out of jail for petty robbery. He copped a plea
(to avoid the Death Penalty, I was at the trial) and is now serving
two consecutive lifetimes, no parole, at xxxxx xxxx. She immediately
hooked up with another guy (called killing the messenger I believe) and
never spoke to me again. They (brother and sister) were both adopted
and I was pretty sure (from her evasions) that she'd been raped by him
as a child repeatedly. Private story. Well, everyone that knew me then
knows it. But I have a hard time—

20.

Out of the cradle endlessly—shameful—out of the rocking the mocking-bird's throat—bludgeoned the musical, the musical shuttle—out of the parents the child from bed—wandered alone, bare-headed, barefoot—wider than—the sleeping suburban—the shower'd halo, sky, sky—one with a golf club, one with the shadows—side by side and blue to blue—twining and twisting as if they were alive—brother and sister memories of birds—your memories, sad brother—of sickness and love—the one the other will absorb—as a child repeatedly, the thence-arous'd words—as syllable for sound, the scene revisits—private story, a little boy—the one the other will include—but I have a hard time, and you beside—

21.

NOTE SPAT

Note unfolded

Note torn from the lap of myself
f.

22.

SHORT LAMENT

This made of light and time

   //compass

            Today I danced with Collin   the Charleston
                                                fluid, exalted, and fine

         as if a dream from years ago.

In the darkened doorway of a theater, my mother lay sleeping or ill.

To get in, I

            stepped over her, stepped

over.

Inside, The Trojan Women. Children playing children
sat on their chubby feet, kneeling with their ankles crossed

            not in pain, not.

The women wept even as they spoke, digging in the earth

                           My mother in the doorway,
face hidden in the rotten ground.

23.

The idea to write a book "about" violence. "What kind?" "The close-up kind."

Because I cannot write the words "school shootings" into the little search box.

Later I hear that whatever you write into the little search box will somewhere
be recorded as data in order to better sell you.

What does the person searching school shootings want to buy?

I keyed "guns" instead, but I don't want to buy a gun.

I could buy a gun.

24.

Tail of fox, nose of rabbit, haunch of weasel,

neck of swan, tail of squirrel, spine of horse.

The boy's face glows like the atom bomb, happy-screen on his lap.

When I say violence, I mean his foot.

Or face.

Newborn hares, fully furred with open eyes.

Meadow mice in grass and weeds.

From rooftop to basement, I am sick of my tongue in my mouth.

Envy animals and liars their beautiful eyes.

25.

SURVIVOR: *for* **ONE TAKEN**

A.

The door opens and Charlie and Amy enter like a perfect comment on our apocalypse fixated time. While sausage cooks below, footsteps in the snow.

The door opens and Charlie and Amy, *pretty in the light now, prettier than trees:*
a perfect ornament for our apocalypse-fixated time. Footsteps in the snow.

Her no-hand over her no-face.

B.

According to my watch, it is too late to begin the calls.
(Winter blue, don't go away, I hunger for your refusals.)

There's a way the sun wakes me. On the bus something moves. Drips from the tip of an icicle, glorious antennae glinting wet. It's that gas station part of her, the *missing* part—

We lost her for good at a truck stop in Denver. That night, the church, cold, grand (*cold* and *grand*), the morning tender somewhere.

The horizon, yellow and solid, comes forward unimpeded
like skin healing over a wound,

like a swelling, reflective wave.

26.

Cold and grand, rare and red:

    I said, "No one steals children, there is nothing to be afraid of."

    The remnants of winter are ugly: torn plastic, two months under
        snow,

                flutters now in a March wind.

My girl climbs a tree; a man in a car watches her. I look up and he looks away.
A friend goes to jail for a night. There she meets another woman who threw a
box of spaghetti at her husband. The box broke and a piece of spaghetti went
into their daughter's eye. Now she is jailed for child abuse. Another one, five
months pregnant, says the prison does not recognize her pregnancy. "Oh, my
baby just moved," she says.

                There is no place outside the world.
                         (Nancy)

27.

BLIND

Hello,

You were no longer missing, but instead gone blind. Blind and silent. Your mother opened the door for me and gestured toward your room. There where you were. I took your hands and put them to my face. They sat on my face. You had no will to move them. Your mother said you were losing your mind. I offered to find a psychiatrist, but she declined. Made lunch.

What does *blind* mean?

If 1/100th are in prison, I cannot see us.

Imagine bread dough. To knead it you must flatten and fold, flatten and fold.

Always much is hidden within the fold.
But the outside and the inside keep trading places
under your hands.

Until later, the knife.

28.

BOMB ARCHIVE

Links:

Alcohol, Anarchy, Bad Ideas, Cars, Computers, Crime, Drugs, Electronics, Fake ID, Fraud, Government/Police, Handbooks, Humor, Hypnotism, Happy, Interrogation, Interior, Lock Picking, Misc, Phreakin, Phones, Revenge Pranks, Rushes, Safety, Spy, Survival, Survival, Weapons and Combat, Zines.

29.

About human dignity and heavy clouds just above the horizon

but spitting out

flames

About rubber bands and tape

About into the cold and

eddies gunbeautiful

You don't have to make something cry. In summer you'll hear them sobbing into their cells
About—classrooms acquire better locks. About

snipers in black with devices for spying snipers in black are dangerous are dangerous /
About

YOUR MOTHER'S HAIR IS TACKED TO THE WALL

30.

feet like little suns

bent around my head

what I cannot write

hay in his heart

crawl into my face

It's really absurd

This is just a book. It does not weigh very much. It is easy to hold and to destroy. Scissors, a knife, a pen, coffee, water, your hands. Like a body.

Sleep with arms around my children, as if—

31.

And here I must add the part about the (Wait. Wait longer) Capitol Hill Rapist. We heard about it when we got here from many different people. He'd walk into houses in the middle of the day and rape whomever he found there: men and women, boys and girls.

Only yesterday did someone tell us he stabbed them too. One boy we know, now eight, then five, saw a woman run naked from a house, screaming and bleeding, she died on the street.

His parents said, "She had an ow-y and she fell down."

32.

The useless mother's face is green, like a blade
of cut grass, sticks

to your
foot

Her voice cold candid flat,
the Atlantic Ocean, a credit

card, that

empty

33.

That empties—his is the voice that—empties—the step that
doesn't, does not, fall—cry of a

baby—the babies all the babies locked in their chunky
car seats—whose is the voice that—rocks endlessly—from out of the—

endlessly empty—uselessly useless foolishly rocking—mine is the
hand that—came shining or knocking or just walking

by—care for can you—you in your slouch your "is that your
baby?"—"yes?"—"I almost stepped on her, I might have hurt her!"—

locked in their rocking their bouncy chunky—I might have—
whose is the foot that—broadens—wide the sky don't—be absurd I—
almost hurt

her

34.

BOMB ARCHIVE 2

Ajax Bomb: This bomb is virtually harmless to you unless you breath in to much of the Ajax powder. [sic]

Bic Flame Thrower: How to make a flame-thrower out of a bic lighter.

Bird Shit Bomb: How to make a shit-spraying bomb. Interesting.

Building A Campo Bomb: Here are the plans to make a nice bomb that is sure to impress your friends.

Acetylene Balloon Bomb: Imagine this. A great, inflated, green garbage bag slowly wafting down from a tall building. It gains some speed as it nears the ground. People look up and say, "What the....?" The garbage bag hits! *BOOM!!!* It explodes in a thundering fireball of green bits of plastic and flame! "What is this?" you may ask. Well, this is the great "Acetylene Balloon Bomb." And here is how to make it.

35.

CONSIDER THIS

Consider this: what is violence? the narrowest hinge between lovers and lamps? trashcans and trains? music and muscle? between pillow and plan? weed and wretched? get this, people, there's nothing wrong with a little defense! no reason to be ashamed of sticking up for yourself! stems of leaves slip into the gutter. in and out and in and out and. the light bulb drinks. fire until sunrise. short stem of morning, what *wrong* with him. just walk away. but walk away quickly. consider hot days in the project pool. "lucky" because we had carpet and coke. a woman's breasts are an upside down heart. not at all. we were not at all safe. he wanted to liquefy the self's solidity / within the body of another. because where else? wind, consider it. it's coming from the west. it's carrying a factory smell. we did not know whether, after passing out in the alley, they recovered. // rum in the coke bottles of twelve-year-old boys. what is penitent? what kind? dazzling and tremendous.

"how quickly the sun rise would kill me if I could not now and always send sunrise out of me." this crewless ship stalled in the shoal: what a project. it's an echo-y stairwell. what is well? what wet? the race-riots of childhood. the projects of broken. here's a wander-site: dump-dogs and "boyfriends" with bruises and boils. pimples and penises. light bulbs drink / in corners and causeways. smoking children. dirt-bike riding children. copulating children. children with their pants down. children with their feet bruised. with their hair a mess. eating children. children in school but hiding. in school but running. in school but can't reach. cars with children and houses with children and dumpsters. enough. return:

honey / suckle and candy / bag. and the window drinks. drinks, not impatient, the body is cut. the body is steering. consider the man / fingering his cock slow-driving alongside us. what's *wrong* with him. dump-dogs and boyfriends. asking directions. consider the disdain / of twelve-year-old girls. our huffy walk home. what is violence. nodding out on a borrowed couch. what we didn't get then we do get now. memories tutor / one another. we were not at all safe. consider harm. not what animals do. the fire-assed monkeys, slow-trunked elephants, decorative zebras, meaty lizards. adjective noun, adjective noun, get the pain out of the hand and put it on the page. "Tenderly—be not impatient, / (Strong is your hold, O mortal flesh, / Strong is your hold O love.)" drink not impatient, the body cut. what hand of the man. so wild in the kitchen. not at all. we were not at all safe. moments of / what is a zebra, what is a meerkat? what is a baby, blinking and wrapped? not at all safe. what is my son?

36.

The ghost said hello to me. I heard him and stood still. Looked around.

> Hello, I said back. If you need to talk to me, find a way to do that without scaring me, I instructed. Like a mother.

37.

Love,

> I threw all the shoes. All of them, even the cleats. Not *at* anyone.

> The baby on your knee watched me, not visibly disturbed. Mothers throw shoes, she thought, ok. The other two hid in their rooms.

> *Sorry, sorry, sorry, sorry, sorry.*

From sore: distressed

> districtus:

> > busy; having many claims on one's attention; pulled

> in different directions

38.

LAUNCED

And now this: her boyfriend is shot and killed in Mexico while trying to protect his mother's purse, so she stops coming to class. "To tell you the truth, my head is just spinning, and I don't know what to do with myself."

Along comes something—launched in context, writes Lyn. But each time I copy it down I lose the "h":

Launced.

This is what happens to the boy then—he is launced. Or one could say his death is now launced into the context of the town. The town receives the boy's death as a lancing wound and a launched event. To not speak of the parents and the sister // to not, to not at all, think of.

"We love you oh life and we get on your nerves."

39.

SURVIVOR 2

It is too late
to begin the calls

The night

cold and
grand

The
morning
tender
somewhere.

40.

SHOPPING LIST

Touch
Touch
Ajax
The underside
Food
& more food
Spring and
Wire tacks
Hair
Clip
Mirror

41.

Lie down little girl, little laugher, little clown
couchwise or in the sea

Festooned like wind by rain, like the inside of an orange

Lie down little girl, little laughter, little joke,
Little avian

riddle

42.

TWO NARRATIVE POEMS

Stephen cut a grid into his shoulder. This he did not explain by telling me that his uncle once grabbed him by the hair and shoved his face into a full toilet. This same uncle was later found dead on the bottom of a motorboat, floating in a pond, with girly magazines and a gun. Stephen and I swinging in a playground at night, feet swooping up toward branches, grey against the black of the sky. I found the grid sexy, but of course I did. Also, the uncle raped him. This I forgot to say. Various ways of writing that. But also, the uncle. The uncle. And the uncle. He raped him, the uncle. Said, he raped him. Swung on the swings, said, stoned, my uncle, he. We had/have the same birthday. He put headphones on my ears, pressed "play": *Madam Butterfly*, Shostakovich. I had not heard such music.

A boy sat in my office, speaking of poems, his interest in graduate school. We were having the pleasantest conversation imaginable. My office is nothing special, but outside there are blooming trees and lilacs. Then I notice his hands: burn marks, perfectly round, fresh and red, seven or eight per hand. Perhaps he sees me notice, places his hands in his lap. We continue to talk. Over the burns. Above the burns.

43.

Resting hands,

why such silence?

No silence.

Anyone in an alley can "look like a robber."

I miss the ghost. I saw him only twice.

How quick to form attachments the human mind is.

Does a cave frighten me?

An ocean floor?

I'm alone in what seems a net made of vines.

Centuries have passed and

less and less

to say.

44.

Cold and grand. Fresh and red.

Currently, nine women on death row,
three-hundred and sixty-nine men on death row

in Texas.

"Creator! shall I bloom?" (Dickinson)

The women on death row have murdered, in most cases, children,
in most cases, their own.

The men have murdered, in most cases, women.

45.

A novelist calls me brave for writing about violence. This seems a condescending thing to say. A scholar mentions the war, the problem of pleasure, and sips his wine. This a condescending sentence to write. The tulips bow their heads. Ruskin: "All violent feelings have the same effect. They produce in us a falseness in all our impressions of external things, which I would generally characterize as the 'pathetic fallacy.'"

My baby wakes up and I am saved by the winds of chance, says the soldier on returning to his two-story home in Pensacola.

46.

DARE READ

A.

"Long, too long America,
Traveling roads all even and peaceful you learn'd from joys and prosperity only,
But now, ah now, to learn from crises of anguish, advancing, grappling with direst
fate and
                recoiling not,
And now to conceive and show to the world what your children en-masse really
are,
(For who except myself has yet conceiv'd what your children en-masse really are?)
                                                    (Whitman)

B.

Drinking a beer to the
Eye of America
A swallowed bit of foam
Recoiling not
She's stilled in her path
A nine-year-old male
She left to starve
The baby cries in her damp
Leashed dogs in the snow
A swallowed bit
Our children en-masse
A mess of tears and non-words
Ate the wallpaper
For its glue
Sweet glue sweet plaster
And now to conceive

of who but myself?

47.

And during a standard visit to the Emergency Room (stitches in the boy's knee)
you are aware

questions are posed in order to determine whether you, the parent,
are the cause of.

The doctor trained to look, not just at the wound, but also
at you.

48.

NARRATIVE POEM

Then, the bicycle pedal sent spinning

I am hungry, speaks the face

The earth erupts into quivering yellow

"Old tree, what now will you do?" (Schuster)

Slapped my son for fighting

A chair regards me

"Out there" —the evangel!

Slouching home

(his four fur feet, his four fur feet, his four fur feet)

I am small and death is coming, speaks the face

In my garden of earthly delay

Bird and dog struggle for airspace

All cries belong only to the past

Going to and fro upon the earth, walking up and down it

49.

WROTH (Cain *and* Abel)

The oldest son was "wroth" his "countenance fell"

He became
a fugitive and a vagabond on earth.

Going to and fro upon the earth, walking up and down it

Out of the—the earth's open mouth—a bulb set to—"Creator! shall I bloom?"

Says Tim, right, your life strewn with dead bodies, all those bleeding in the street. But, I say, violence is everywhere. Everywhere, he answers, right. The ordinary food, paper, tape, the face of a dog, mums, just blanketing. We were sitting on the porch. Our kids and our friends' kids running in and out of the house. Early fall. Still green. A man and a woman approached. Ordinary clothes. But they were wearing rubber gloves. "Hello." "Hi?" "Have you seen a body?" they asked this, "in a garbage bag?" Of course, we stared at them. Didn't know that we'd heard right. Then we noticed other people walking the street, crossing the avenue. Rubber gloves. "She is known to be in a garbage bag." "Three years old." They are parting bushes, peering into dumpsters. Go away. The children in and out of the house: Ben and Alice, Kat and Marina, Joe and Henry. Go away. And the baby in her stroller, sleeping.

50.

My son is wroth. Dear summer, dear aging, the bottoms of cups:

If bearing children is a game one plays
with fate and

is a joke: trees as yet unleaved, a sunny——

My son is wroth, my daughter too, and me, myself, I am wroth. A fugitive

on the earth, and a vagabond. Dear opposition, dear trashed strollers, dear

torn to pieces: Wasn't, won't be, isn't me

collecting swords, hanging them on my living room wall, that's my

neighbor, he's recording God-songs, God-songs for the radio, suited up for

long red nights in the God-studio.

Their ordinary clothes, their rubber gloves: "Have you seen a body?

Have you seen one?"

51.

DARE READ 2

> "Why are you shuddering? Yes, I was laughing at you! I had been insulted, just before, at dinner, by the fellows who came that evening before me. I came to you, meaning to thrash one of them, an officer; but I didn't succeed, I didn't find him; I had to avenge the insult on someone to get back my own again; you turned up, I vented my spleen on you and laughed at you. I had been humiliated, so I wanted to humiliate; I had been treated like a rag, so I wanted to show my power…" (Dostoevsky)

She slapped me and I was pleased.

He took me by the arms and shook me.

I called him a prick and a loser.

She locked herself in the bathroom and remained silent for three hours.

He grabbed my breast when we shook hands.

I had been treated like a rag, as I lay there on the floor, she kicked me in the
    stomach.

I looked at my child's face and I slapped it.

He put his knees on the inner parts of my elbows and held me there.

A bit of drool stretched from his mouth, headed for mine. I turned my face,
    shut my eyes.

He climbed through the window while I was asleep.

She threw the pot of boiling water at his stomach.

She threw the cutting board at my foot and it broke on the floor in front of me.

They placed the trashcan next to me and called it a wedding.

They pulled him out of his wheelchair, tried to throw him in the trash, but he was
    too heavy.

I made her hang from her arms until she fell. Then I did it again.

We followed the old woman home, taunting her, whispering things at the back of
    her head.

I lifted her from where she stood and threw her on to the bed. Like a rag.

And I was pleased.

They left him on the floor.

He put his hand over my mouth, tried to pull the sheet from between us.

He ran out of the room, looking for him, he would "trash" him if he could find
    him.

She screamed at him again and we hid, hugging each other, behind the couch.

He pulled me onto the bed and "tickled" me until I cried.

She slammed the car door on my thumb. To avenge the insult.

52.

NOTE DISCARDED

Lament every this.

I feel happy.

Sky of mathy clouds.

53.

FLORIDA

This is a pretty day. Pools and chairs. Blue and steady.
                        Day rows itself from itself

at me

This is a pretty day. Cups and chairs. Blue and steady.

                Where's my plug-in? Where's my piece of charge? My grid?

I'm
                against forests of falling and fevers of calling.

This Florida sun, this Florida gated:

                sugar-ants in the kitchen, gecko at the sill. This is a pretty day.

                (Where's my mother-no-longer? One less one to call. You think
                this sentimental? But I've got more sentiment than I can spell.)

                (Chairs cocked, leaning on the table edge—tired drunks)

    Stood on one side of a door, heard fighting on the other, someone yelling into a

cell, *don't*
                do this don't do this, sobbing into a cell, one car driving by.

Daylight is for children but nighttime is for
                        mad. Pools and chairs, cells and chargers,

T shirts and water, water and salt.

I said, I'm against the felling and against showing my

        card, this Florida, this gated.

Woman reading, puts down her book, says: "I don't know what it is, but I just

        don't trust him, can't trust that man's face, don't know what it is," said,
        quieter now, *whispering*, "I'm just not trusting a black man," says, "forgive

        me, but I'm *not*."

Children jumpy, bouncy at the elevator, ready to board: good water-sounds, good sun-
feel, good

        flowers stuck on blooming, rowing

        at me, a kind of to-be-born.

54.

MOTHER and DAUGHTER DREAMS

I woke up for the baby, her face dripping sweat. Wiped her down with the sheet. Then I noticed a light on in the kitchen. Stood to turn it off. Heard a sound, running

water, someone   filling a glass. Had to gather up my lungs, actually suck the air, in order to shout: "Get out!" Waited. Then an answer, and footsteps, someone coming up. Began to cry.

so I ask,t my mother if I colde get a horse but she side no so I went to my room
I din,t like her enser so I went to my brother,s and step,t on a legow. first I side
kleen up then I side and go to bed
bbbbbbbbbbbbbbbbbbbbbbbbbbbbbbbbbbbbbbbbbbbbbbbbbbbbbbbbbbbbbbbbbb
bbbbbbbbbbbbbbbbbbbbbbbbbbbbbbbbbbbbbbbbbbbbbbbbbbbbbbbbbbbbbbbbbb
bbbbbbbbbbbbbbbbbbbbbbbbbbbbbbbbbbbbbbbbbbbbbbbbbbbbbbbbbbbbbbbbbb
bbbbbbbbbbbbbbbed

55.

A POEM BY ALICE (Age Six)

Early every evening she sits on the steps of her porch.

She has a baby in the trailer, biking on a caterpillar.

Eyes drink from hot wine. A hot tongue gets wine

and the eyes turn it hot.

And the person is mad, alright, she's mad.

56.

I am a sick man. I am a spiteful man. I am an unattractive man. I believe my liver is
     diseased. (Dostoevsky)

Actually, he, Alexander, was innocent. Wasn't he? (Acker)

We know he was made, like all of us, from a moment of sexual intension.

I want a horse, but I *am* a horse.

Or intrusion. A moment of intrusion.

I am a sick man. A spiteful man.

"Where have you been, sister?" "Killing swine." (*Macbeth*)

A man and his family are driving to a vacation spot. Once a writer, now insurance broker with two kids in the back, wife beside him, map open on her lap. It's hot. They stop at a gas station so the kids can pee, the wife can buy some gum. Gas up. In the gas station bathroom the man catches another man's face in the mirror. For a moment his heart pounds. Something like desire. But this passes. The man is someone he knew in college. Not possible! It is! And they grin, almost embrace. How are you? What are you doing? Etc. The man walks his friend to the car, introduces him to his wife and kids. The kids take little notice. The wife smiles but seems impatient. It is decided that the man will follow along in his car, will join the family for dinner when they arrive at their destination. During the three-hour's drive, the first man tells his wife all about his friend: antics, parties. Why, she thinks, have I never heard of this man before? As evening falls, they arrive at the hotel—old and worn-down, concrete and carpet—not far from the North Carolina coastline. Dump their bags in the room, kids jump beds, they head down to the restaurant where the friend is waiting for them. He smiles and rises when they—

57.

Mottled pigeons not in this city but squirrels on haunches some rabid.
Light bulbs and driers vans and paper cups gorgeous plentitude decay.

My breasts under my shirt: bloody and milky substances kept apart.
I don't believe in the bonds of blood, I like kids for one hour, says a friend.

Another, as he clambers on top of me, I won't hurt you, shush, shush.
My mother kicked my shin and I kicked her back. Why did I so enjoy this?

Later, my stepfather hid the knives. To protect himself, to protect her.

58.

MORE SHOPPING

Gunaccessories.com is pleased to offer one of the world's largest selection of firearm accessories, gun parts, tactical gear, police equipment, Gerber knives, Buck knives and an assortment of upgrades for handguns, rifles, shotguns, Ar-15 and ak-47 military style guns. Our vast selection of gun parts includes barrels, grips, magazines, clips, bolts, hammers, barrel bushings, springs, recoil pads, recoil buffers, mag wells, mainspring housings, sights, scope mounts, slide components, extractors, ejectors, triggers, sears, pins, pistol grips and frontstraps. I want a horse and I am a horse.

Our selection of Gun Parts will fit handgun and rifles manufactured by Armalite, Auto Ordnance, Beretta, Browning, Bond Arms inc., Bushmaster, Chricket, Charter Arms, Colt, Comanche, European American Armory, Firestorm, Glock, Hastings, Hi-Point, Legacy Sports, Magnum Research, Mossberg, Navy Arms, New England, North American Arms, Phoenix, Ruger, Savage Arms, Snake Charmer, Spartan Gun Works, Taurus, Tikka, Verona, Walther Handguns and Weatherby. I want a horse and I am a horse.

Military style rifle owners will be pleased with the massive selection of components and accessories for Ak-47 and Ar-15 style rifles. Items include barrels, bolt carriers and assemblies, buttstocks, folding stocks, free float tubes, handguards, flashiders, muzzle brakes, flash hiders, gas tubes, gas blocks, bayonets, receiver covers, and match sights. Ak-47 builds are very popular and we carry U.S. compliance parts for building Ak-47 rifles and Ak-47 pistols as well as dress up parts for your favorite Ak-47. Ar-15 rifles are again readily available as well as Ar-15 pistols.

I want one and I am one.

In addition to the firearm items and gun parts, we carry a large selection of Knives from leading manufacturers such as Almar Knives, Anza Knives, Benchmade Knives, Browning Knives, Chef's choice, Cold Steel, Columbia

River knife & Tool, Hen & Rooster, Ka-Bar Knives, MOD, Spyderco, Tomahawk Brand, Wyoming knife Corp., United Cutlery, EZE Lap.

Want, am.

59.

The book about violence must be a book of quotations.
For everyone speaks about violence.
Is a book of memories, for everyone's life is riddled.

Whereas the floating hand of sexual love stirs the baby's within, the floating arms of Godly love lift the earth to the sun. Whereas trees by the river greening. Girls in the coffee line, ravened and foamed.

Precise in their aging, the bodies roam. Not every day's a happy day; my plays are peppered with crime.

       Agree,

               agree to take me with you.

60.

Man goes constantly in fear of himself. (Bataille)

Let us accept the dead in their irrevocable 'situation.' By what right can we suspect them of actions that, under other circumstances and in face of other pressures, they might have committed? No, we cannot look for the murderer among *them*. (Wiesel)

Tenderly—be not impatient, / (Strong is your hold, O mortal flesh, / Strong is your hold O love.) (Whitman)

The sight or thought of murder can give rise to the desire for sexual enjoyment for the neurotic anyway. (Bataille)

Others wonder if our lack of success at contacting other forms of higher life, despite an array of satellites and detection equipment, could possibly mean that higher life forms destroy themselves and that extreme violence, a by-product of intelligence, has obliterated them. (Dutton)

Cathy: convicted of the murder of the 3-month-old Brandon B. had been babysitting the boy and his 2-year-old brother.

Cruelty is only the negation of the self, carried so far that it is transformed into a destructive explosion: insensitivity makes the entire being tremble. (Blanchot)

Violence akin to vim: strength; and to vaya: meal.

I'm on a mission. I can't stop.

But ah, but O thou terrible, why wouldst thou rude on me /Thy wring-world right foot rock? (Hopkins)

Now I will do nothing but listen. (Whitman)

61.

COLORADO

Colorado has the highest rate of teen depression in the nation. Believe it. In a class of thirteen 19–20-year-olds, two are bipolar, two are alcoholic, one can't wake up, one's best friend has just been shot. Sores around their mouths. Skin burned red. One misses class, bailing her friend out of jail. Another's being stalked and must get a court order. Kid you not. Most are on meds. Sunny skies. Lots of skiing. Who can account? Littleton Colorado, whereof the Columbine Massacre, is an unimpressive suburb. But pretty. Mountains in the distance. Lots of skiing. Lots of churches. Sad, sad mothers and fathers.

I'm done. Done doing this and doing that and saying this and saying that I'm done. Done for and done in, done doing for and being done to. Under delicate bits of dust, I swim backwards. Now that's a trick. If you must make a racket, do it somewhere else, someone said. Someone said, Everything I do is a text. I filter my life through the text of my face. That's big, someone answered, that's really big. Wanna share a foot-long? No, I can't do that. Someone said, this should be put on hold, but later, somewhere, we'll come upon its true sense. Someone said, I cannot enter normal places, but instead stand outside, tapping on store windows. It has something to do with the heat. Something to do with the wayward. She ran down the street in her heels, sobbing as he pursued her. As soon as I'm done here, I'm going to fall asleep. Do I have no stamina? None whatsoever. Did you own a gun? Never did. And why didn't you? It was redundant, he says. *Quiet, quiet, still.* Said, want that well-done or rare? But what could be more rare than you?

Than you, sad mother, sad father?

62.

The sun hurts. It's hard to grow old. It's hard to relax. He's right. Too many chairs here. (Hanna)

Saw a newborn on a couch. Slit eyes and rising belly. No commerce.

Sleep hit me

directly in the face

63.

AVID

A.

The moss of subjectivity (Guest)

      spreading side-wise like spilled milk

    and it's myself I'm afraid of with my dress made of coffee, dress made of wax, dress of ink, of

        recoil and delay

Consider this:

      (Creator, shall I
            more walled now than walking?
            more stunted than speaking?)

An 8-year-old in Arizona on trial for killing his father and his father's friend.

"Vincent Romero was no stranger to guns / The avid hunter reportedly asked his priest whether he should buy his young son a firearm."

"That child, I don't think he knows what he did," said the Very Rev.

    John Paul Sauter.

      (That child—One wants—   )

"It's an unusual case," Murphy told Maggie. "We hear about 8-year-olds accidentally shooting a gun. This was execution. So I venture it's fair to say // there was something pretty awful going on behind closed doors."

I venture—Fair to say—Give a child a gun and you might get shot, you fucking—

The avid hunter: the avidly dead.

Daylight's coming, but not for you. No, no, not for you.

B.

Creator, shall I

swallow all the guns and like Tikki Tikki Tembo No Sarimbo fall gun-
heavy into the well? Shall I swallow all of them? Shall I

neon open

swing to cirrus, finger

the beautiful

bus ride?

That girl I'm seated next to, I could make her cry. It's easy to discern the fault lines in her face. Sun rising into purple sky and a man talking to himself, increasingly agitated, increasingly avid: I don't have fucking time for this, fuck that, he says. First they tell me this bus, then that fucking bus. *Fuck* you, he says, I want to *fuck* someone right now. The woman beside him, jaw tightening, hard window-staring, that purple purple.

There's never been one day that I was innocent. Not one.

Creator, get me open, get me bloomed and / get me wasted.

64.

FROM GENERAL TO SPECIFIC

A.

First, the premise: When people feel their freedoms encroached upon, they will hurt whoever seems to be encroaching. Upon.

For instance, when there is too much laundry, the clothes seem to be eating me. My arms and my hands are not my own, I cannot move from the spot. In this moment I begin to grow hot. And once, twice, more times, I lifted my hand to hit, I threw the phone, a book, a shoe.

But, some argue, there is no real and unbreachable boundary between people. When we finally recognize the absence of boundaries, we will, in fact, no longer hurt one another, because to do so would be to hurt ourselves, they say.

Quite the opposite seems to be true. A lack of boundaries means I can do just exactly what I want to you. Just as Michael cut a grid into his arm, I can cut one into yours. I am a sick man. I am a spiteful man.

If it is profitable to burn / kiss my own / your hand, how do I measure this profit?

B.

My mother was afraid of crowded trains. She had to ride the hot crowded train from the center of the city to our house on the outskirts every day. Hot in summer. Hot in winter. Standing up, holding on, other bodies bumping hers, sometimes pressing. And she was very short; likely she could not see past the backs or chests of the men and women surrounding her. This situation reminded her of the trains in Europe carrying the Jews to their deaths. You know of this: the people dying while standing. The body does not fall because so tightly packed; it slumps, instead, against another. The children and the toddlers, slumped, the mothers. So that when she got home, she was frightened. Her eyes were frightened, moving quickly, and wide, just as they would become permanently quick and wide once her mind began to lose itself. And if the dishes were in the sink, this fear would turn. Here I stop. Why tell you this? Do you pity the children hiding in their rooms, unable to come down the stairs? I do not pity these children; pity their mother.

65.

I came to the conclusion that the most powerful human emotion by far.

The subject of this book is fear; the subject of this book causes fear. (Dutton)

And he walked around the globe on his four fur feet, his four fur feet, his four fur feet.

It may start with attachment to the mother, and indifference to all who are not her. (Dutton)

First, the premise: When people emerge from a de facto partition they are drawn under
   wraps.

First, the premise: When people chant their own abstract name, they find themselves in a sea
   of flags.

The premise: When people inspire followers and cow opponents, slow-witted slothful
   launched into action.

The subject of this book is self-willed individuals, the theft of a bottle of wine.

I came to the conclusion, "though you look so passive, ample and spheric, there, / I now
   suspect that is not all." (Whitman)

I came to the conclusion that I'd considered too long, too long the ocean, too too long the
   shore.

I came: I "breathed enough," the "lungs are stirless, must descend." How cool, how cool.
   (Dickinson)

How cool the bellows feels! (Dickinson)

The conclusion: will live with their loved ones in everlasting bliss. Too deep, the ocean, too
   long, the shore.

The premise: When people are drawn into sentences made of scales and arrows, stymied by the complexities, there is no way out.

Squirrel on the roof, ants in the sink, mouse in the pipe, mold in the curtain, the bellows.

67.

MOTHER AND DAUGHTER 2

sweetkickI'llkillyouIAMnotcrazydon'tcallmec
razyohstupidrightyouthinkI'mstupidfuckyouf
uckyouI'mnotstupidI'MAnicepersoniceper
sonIknowyouwantadifferentmotheranIcemo
mmyanicemommygetawayfrommejustgoaw
ayyayayayayathat'sallyousaytheNOiseisjustban
gbanbangbangI'mnotstupidwhydoyouthinkI'
msostupidmISerablejustmiserableI'Msomise
erablenotstupiddOn'tcallmestupidorcrazyI'mn
otcrazyyou'recrazyNOMomyou'renotcrazyn
obody'scallingyoucrazyyou'reverysmartwelov
eyouhiMomMomHiAliceiscomingBenhe'sco
mingtooremember Ben? Mom I'mhavingababy
Momshshshshsshshs   I   crazyOhIknowall
youwanttodoiskil   going to let you kill
megetawayfromme Oh yeah I wasanicepersonI
wasnicebutnotnownownotnicejuststupidIkno
wwhatyousayaboutmeblablablabalNoMomw
wedon'tMomlookMomtheriverTheriverisprettyt
hat'stheCharlesriverwhydon'tyoujustkillejus
tkillmeinsteadoFALLthistalkingstoptalkingorI
'lljustkillMomlet'ssinglet'ssingForSpacious
SkiesyourememberamericaamericaGodshed
hisGraceontheeorweshallovercomeremember
WeShallOvercoouoomweshallovercoouuuoo
mpurplemountainsthat'srightMAjestyandAM
berwavesofgrainAMericaAMericagodshedhis
graceontheeyoulikethatoneshouldwesingitaga
in?Iknowlet'sdobluemoonrememberBlueMoo
n?Bluemoonohiforgetthewordsstupidstupidw
hyaretheyallcallingmestupid?Ohyouyouyouth
at'srightyouhateMENOnoMomwedon'twant
todance?Let'sdancewhatdowehavehere?some
reggae?that'sfinewantacookie?here'sacookie?
wantanothercookie?thosearegooduckyouyou
justwatchoutbecauseIhateyouwhyareyoutalki
ngaboutme?whyareyoulookingatme?whydoy

77

68.

Here's a happy place.

Sun on rooftops. Sun in blue. Hissy happy foam.
Nothing so safe as the sun.

Nothing so safe as blue.

"Fire safety officers inspected the furnace and gave it the all-clear.

It is easy to cast this as negligence, but council workers checking a furnace can hardly be expected to be on the lookout for buried families." (BBC News)

For imprisoning his daughter and (so safe as the) raping her for 24 (car the yard the) fathering six (blue) by her, and (in and out and in and out and) imprisoning (what is well? what wet?) three (safe as the) he can serve (sun the sun serve the sun) a maximum of 15 (in blue happy blue) years.

sun so safe, safe in the car, safe in the yard

whereas my mouth

whereas my vagina. whereas my nipples. whereas my eyes.

69.

A million, billion fishes   trace the swirly whirly wet

        tongueless, lidless fishes

nick the sunlight with their scales.

Once I had a girl on Rocky Top, half bear, other half cat

    wild as a mink, but sweet as soda pop

I still dream about that.

70.

I read my materials and I wanted

                                to fuck. Therein I found

the pleasure principle, therein I found

                                      something new: I began to see

bodies as split

                                  under their clothes they can be torn

like paper dolls.

There was something else: I wanted to

                                  hold my baby so none would

hurt her. Whereas I'll

                                  do and I'll do and I'll do

Whereas there were two lives   —one in which the little girl and I

dance: the rose, the lilacs, tulips, the phone rings

                              ring

            ring   ring ring ring

And the other in which

                                  nothing breathes

nothing at all

71.

ANOTHER NARRATIVE POEM

In recent days, Mr. Shaw has found himself able to recount, somewhat matter of factly,/the ordeal of hearing the pop of gun shots, opening the front door and seeing his son on the sidewalk/in a pool of blood, bits of head scattered near his fallen iPod. // But then he opens his car trunk and sees the half-empty bottle of cranberry juice his/son discarded before a recent football practice, and Mr. Shaw finds his breath gone,/consumed by the tugging agony of loss. // "Every day I just see that boy laying in the street dead," he said, sobbing. "I just want to get/him back. That's why I can't stop. I'm on a mission. I can't stop."

(*New York Times*, May 15, 2008)

72.

QUESTIONS and GAMES

Can I recycle this? Does postmodernism mimic the apocalypse? Do you need the car? Do you want to come? If those are your shoes, why is my hair in your hand? Where is your face? Does the instrument land on the nerve? Your wife is asleep? Is that your baby? Can you? Move? Over?

Pigeon rope tightening: tightly binding a prisoner with his/her arms drawn up behind them by rope in such a manner that the victim is unable to move his/her body.

Clock torture: standing on one leg with both arms stretched out to mirror the hands of a clock and the other leg swinging like the pendulum of a clock.

Motorcycle torture: forcing a prisoner to imitate for hours on end the physical motions of riding a motorcycle, and endlessly repeating the process of sitting down and standing up. (Human Rights Watch)

If God is mimetic in voice and body, do you want room for cream?
If at birth surrounded by ox and donkey, preorder now?

73.

DREAM ESSAY

I hear on the radio that the Swiss soldier has been captured and shot. But it is my job to take him to see his mother. I am a nurse, though I am also much more than that. I hold his hand and we walk to the building where she is being kept. Together we sit on the sidewalk and look up at the windows. "Is that her?" I ask, shining my light on a woman in a nightgown, short wisps of white hair. "Yes," he says, "that's her." An attendant helps her to rise, hands her a baby doll. "Why does she have a doll?" I ask, though I know why. The soldier's shame is evident. Quietly, "Will they take care of her?" as we rise to leave. "Yes," I answer, though I know she will be killed, just as he has been.

"There," I say, "you can get away! Run down those stairs. Just go, go now." He runs down the subway stairs. He rides his skateboard down the subway stairs. He rides his waterboard down the waterstairs. He stands at the top and sends his board and his waterboard down the waterstairs to see which is faster. The woman in the token booth is on the phone, is saying, "A Swiss soldier?" and looking at him, peering at him; he grabs his boards and he runs.

He is my son, my son Benjamin, and we must get him to safety. It's dusk in New York City. We take turns pushing the baby in her stroller. Alice walks, holding our hands, and we also carry an ear of corn wrapped in a blanket like a newborn. Tim's mother has an apartment on 41st Street; she is preparing a birthday party for Benjamin and if we can get him there, he will be safe. I can see the balloons, but we cannot find her building. We know New York City, we lived here years ago, but we cannot find Amsterdam Avenue. Avenues have names we've never heard of—Fishman, Turner. And the numbers will not behave consecutively. We are on 23rd Street and have only 18 blocks to go. But 23rd leads to 36th, 36th to 40th. We are almost there, I tell everyone, shifting the corn in my arms. But now we're on 21st again. Something has happened; the avenue has turned?

No, I understand. It's because he is already dead. But he must not know this, he must not be told. The sun is going down. Ravening clouds, the burial clouds, black masses spreading.

74.

Up since three, pain in the hip, the elbow, the wrist:
sweet pain, sweet for mild, sourced to no true threat.

But why has sexual want been taken? Why no longer the pleasures of—

I cannot love children

    (feet like little suns, gathered around a table, honeysuckle halos)

At the new museum: paintings of bloodied horses, of houses with their roofs blown
off, a man without eyes, without

enough. Can't love them enough.

                                the back of his head.

                  I could never run for president. I'm far too sick of—

75.

THREE MOTIVES

A.

When I was.
Once when I.
Tied to a.
Drove the car.
Fell to his knees.
Pretty pretty pretty.
Now so wary.
Shook the shutter.
From the outside.
Days spent alone.
I've never wanted.
Pretty pretty.
Don't touch my.

B.

In the abridged version of William T. Vollmann's *Rising up and Rising Down: Some Thoughts on Violence, Freedom and Urgent Means,* there is a series of photographs which Vollmann calls "Weapons on Parade." Of the 28 people photographed with their weapons, most are boys, no girls, only one is a woman. To my knowledge no one has ever been able to explain why women have so much less interest in weapons than do men. Obvious jokes aside, it seems universally true and universally mysterious. But this is not to say that girls and women are not violent. The most direct violence I have known was perpetrated by my mother who never used a weapon, though she sometimes threw things. My daughter too will hit, will often threaten to "poke your eye out," but will never pick up a stick to swing at you. Perhaps females are the more violent for using their hands, are more prepared for the pure contact of hand to body? I was beaten by a group of girls I did not know. They knocked me to the ground, and one sat on me and slammed my face again and again with her fist. When she was finished, she stood up and kicked me twice in the stomach. It was, in fact, a satisfying experience because before this happened, I was afraid. Afterwards, I was not. To be punched in the face (by a fifteen-year-old girl) turned out not to hurt all that much. My mother was horrified when she saw me—she cried as she wiped the blood from my face. But this was nothing compared to the ways she had hurt me with the things she said. Later, when my daughter screamed at me because I'd removed the baby from her rough grip, I answered with what I hope sounded like deep sarcasm, "Go ahead and pack." I knew, of course, that it was possible she would remember this, possible that it would hurt her for years to come. And in that moment, I did not care. Clearly it is far worse to be rejected by one's own mother than it is to be beaten by strangers. Even the man who climbed into my window and came very close to raping me did not hurt me as much as my mother did when she said she hated me. Even as he pushed his hand over my mouth, knees on my elbows, and even as I tried to bite him, kicked at the air, he was an object of fascination— why was he doing this? And even though for a long time after, sex became something vaguely or not so vaguely repulsive, this was still nothing compared to my mother's insults, though I do not remember them. It took a long time to be able to observe her rage and say to myself, "That has nothing to do with me." And even when, at age ten, I could say this, I am certain I did not believe it. By then she too had become an object of disgust. In defense I imagined my future children, how well I would love them, how calm I would be. In fact, I am not calm. But it is true that they remain the reason I am writing this, the reason I am afraid to write this, and the reason that writing this cannot be the only activity within any day that matters.

C.

Let me back up farther. For what motivates is less one's own grievances than a growing sense that the social world of houses and families, of children and gardens, is scotch tape. Scotch tape. Perhaps it is difficult to peel off, but it is not at all difficult to see the objects and events to which it adheres.

76.

On the night of the day that I learn my good friend was raped by a stranger who had broken into her house, raped at gunpoint when she was 21 while her older brother slept in the next room over, I dreamed my son and I performing a joint suicide. The mood was cheerful. I went first, a letter opener through my temple—clean, swift, and surprisingly painless. And then he did the same. An imperfect circle of blood like a wad of scarlet chewing gum just above his ten-year-old ear. We looked at each other with what felt like happiness and waited for death. When death did not come immediately, he suggested we play Scrabble while waiting. There was a gun and I asked him to pass it to me so I could speed things up. But holding the gun to the back of my head I was suddenly overcome with remorse. I put the gun down and ran my fingers through his hair, now wet with warm blood. Oh Benjamin, what have we done? Is the world not good enough for us?

I cannot get that guy's face out of my mind, she said,

though it's been almost thirty years.

77.

HOLDING HANDS

A.

I've been trying to look *through* the sun

        at something under the sun or within the sun

     (here are the sunny days: 280 a year!) been trying to measure the sun—
taste the sun. But I cannot

           break into the sun.

On the way to the store Alice and I discuss fear.
What do you do if you are alone and you see a robber?
You give him your money and then you run.
What if he wants to steal *you*?
Then you run.
What if he is faster than you?
You find other people, you scream.
What if there are no other people?
Then you shouldn't be there alone.
But what if you are?
Then you run.
What do *you* do if you are alone and you see a robber?
I don't go where there are robbers.
But how do you know? What if that man is a robber?
He's not. See, I'll say hi to him. Hi. See, he's nice.
I'm afraid of him.
I'm not.
Why not?

See that woman in the red dress? Why is she just standing there at the light? Why is she not crossing the street? I am afraid of her. Is she still standing there? Now? Do you think she is still standing there now?

B.

Heat of the oven against my thighs.

I fell down in it.

Perhaps you are laughing? What do I care? My geraniums bounced in
      the breeze and I, like many others, felt justified in spitting

         at the sun.

Why are you so sure that the only defensible life is that of the martyr or the nurse?

My thighs were hot, my hands hot too,

     as if waiting for the final

     touch. Remember,

         holding her hand, I walked my mother
         around and around the construction site.

     Each time we passed the piles of beams, the reams of plastic, we read the
     names of the corporations stenciled on these materials: *Grace, Milton*—

      a pleasure because she still *could* read.

A dog passed us, and we barked at it. It barked back, startling.

And now, in the kitchen, I am free.

78.

Then I began to read police reports.

> "I'm not repentant. I'm not sorry she was raped," he said of one of his victims. "I'm in prison doing 400 years. I don't have time to feel sorry for her."
>
> (Quintin Wortham, "Capitol Hill Rapist")

When her dementia was progressing and she began to grow more violent, more full of rage, my siblings and I debated whether the disease revealed her true character or instead forced her into avenues that, though habitual, were no more truly her than the gentler behavior she seemed to have left behind. Of course, at that point we all tried to forgive her when she swung an arm, slapped my stepfather's back, swore at him, at us. But we still had not forgiven her for the days 30 years ago during which she'd held us in a kind of rigidity.

This question—which "side" of the person is "real"—was, in fact, her question too. When she was in her fifties, she read a series of books on the subject, books about the question of evil, whether it exists, how we are to explain it. God and the devil held no purchase on her, though she enjoyed a popular biography of Jesus in about 1995. But her reading took her nowhere. As an EMT's assistant she witnessed the worst the island she lived on had to offer: a house torn to pieces, a bloodied hand, a bloodied head. No murders, no reported rapes.

> "Wherever you find knots of men
> you will find the charisma of violence." (CD Wright)

> "He said, `No one is crying for me.'" (NPR News)

79.

It's about time to go. That edge-worn jacket
of late winter—and someone's singing up on top of his car

Inside the raw scar on his knee, I place the imagined land of ether and dust.

I'm leaving in the dark—travel is travel to-

                                 ward death.

Under the oily cold semi-urban air, the waking sounds of industry and dogs

dig me in.

80.

SOME MORE RESEARCH!

The boys eating their ice cream on the back porch list favorites. They get three sets of three: three bands, three songs, and three things. They all like the same bands, the same songs, but not the same things. Ben: pasta, Legos, sports. Joe: video games, Baby Lucy, swimming! Kalil: singing, broccoli, video games. Mike: pizza, guitars, guns. His dad's got a sword collection, and, we learn now, a gun one too.

His mother as she leaves kisses his head, "Be a blessing," she says.

And he is.

How cool the bellows.

But then it turns out that all the other dads have gun collections too. And maybe you do as well. And though they keep the guns "locked up," they have licenses to "carry while concealed." But why would they need this? For camping! they explain. We are, we gather, one of only two families, of those represented by the 7 boys, who do not own guns. And so, swiftly it becomes unremarkable. One mother, "I was against it. But then I realized it was a boy thing, and so what could I do?" Another mother, "That's his thing!"

In 2005, 1,972 children and teenagers in the US were murdered with guns, 822 committed suicide with guns, and 173 died in unintentional shootings.

The rate of firearm death of under-14-years-olds is nearly 12 times higher in the US than in 25 other industrialized countries combined.

A 2003 study indicated that the presence of a gun in the home made it 6 times more likely that an abused woman would be murdered than other abused women.

A quick google search on the subject of guns in Colorado after Columbine reveals that the vast majority of published articles defend the citizen's right to own guns and to store them where they might be readily available for self-defense.

The next line of inquiry is to discover how many gun owners have successfully defended themselves or their families against violent attacks within their own homes.

A 12-year-old in North Carolina needs parental permission to play Little League Baseball, but not to possess a rifle or shotgun. In Texas and five other states, there is no minimum legal age requirement for gun possession.

(Brady Campaign)

81.

Enough of that.

Would the talkers be talking? would the singer attempt to sing? (Whitman)

> Oh, Happy Air! (Dickinson)

Some residence—to defend—some Neighbor—some—beat beat beat—upon the rattle—quicker air—heavier blows—dash child—to the fort!—happy air—green green canopy—not to be timid—not to be impeded—

Your violence or mine?—confess entirely?—gospel back of a man—his skin under his shirt—his material possessions—his drink of water—baby who crawls to my leg—what does she know of harm?—what does he?—

The heat of the sun portends the end of the earth—solo on a sax—a shy sassy smile—the made-up eyes of the coffee girl—heat pouring through panes—sugar sludged at the bottom of my cup—man with a knife—took my bike—in the sun in the sun—we are the people on the outside—stupid stuff on the computer—his drink of water—face in the sidewalk, in the cement, speaking upward—on and on and on and on—

The tyranny of two plus two making four, says Dostoyevsky, no one really wants this—this mere logic, this mere reason—sludged at the bottom—head on the desk—sometimes it was too much to lift it—his sister's death pouring through panes—his skin under his shirt—went back home to find her—not finding her in the sun—what does he?—head on the desk again—I said, it's ok if you don't talk, every day—if you never—when did you last kiss the sole of another's foot?—another's sickle-shaped foot?—

82.

whereas my mouth. whereas my vagina. whereas my nipples. whereas my ears. whereas my eyes.

83.

NOTE ON VENGEANCE

If I agree to the terms, if I agree to my cast. If I attempt to see into the ordinary to make it break, to see how it is already broken:

One woman comes daily to drink her coffee, her cup shaped like the head of a pig. Gazes out the window with her pen in her hand: streetlights, headlights, dawn. She'd not seen me in a dozen weeks and came over to say hello: "Joe was talking to a girl. We were fighting a little bit. But the girl was his cousin! I made him so angry he swore at me and grabbed my arm, he threw me down. That's what jealousy does: helps you play games in the worst possible way."

A family had a special anger room, a room to sit in and count. Another had a bell to ring that meant, I cannot speak to you now or I will say something hateful.

In a third family the parents will, at moments of crisis, leave the house, walk the neighborhood, staring at the concrete until something lifts. I'm not thinking logically when day turns to night. Couples dance ankle-deep in a fountain—dance the tango, kick up lit sprays. I'm not looking into mirrors now for fear of another's face. Not recording my dreams. Don't want that radio to speak to me: "My daughter's death must not go un-avenged!" Let the car idle; will the mother say more?

You cannot put a fire out

Pretty is the light now
Prettier than trees

...

Can go itself without a fan
Upon the slowest night
(Dickinson)

84.

But what was I up to?

There was a bush growing skyward really needed pruning, sun getting
stymied and stumped by cloud-stock, like cardstock, so stiff.

There was something to know and no way to know it. What's a normal
living, a protected? Said,

Kids at the pool, at every moment you're going under: blurred and un-
identifiable, said, watch it I told you stay near me stay shallow,

no way to.

Some shit on the men's room floor and my son dropped his pants on it. Un-

protected.

Women stand watching—the curves of their backs, their gently sloping waists.

Then, just as I feared, violence began to seem banal. One student of it, in a
20-year-search, traveled to Korea, Iraq, Beirut, in search of it, carried a gun
in his hometown as if to court it, interviewed the murdered by peering at
their corpses: anything to keep

the smell of it alive.

85.

A FINAL SHOPPING LIST

hands.
melted ice.
sun.
shine.
wire.
wire.
that which can be.
that which cannot.
a strategy.
the end of the day.
the heat at my neck.
sugar high.
the inside of his mouth.
the mother skirt.
hot sidewalk by the DMV.
the buzz in my head.
the fear running up the side of it.
partitions.
balm.
other kinds of balms.
whatever the children want.

86.

THE ILLUSIVE

Hey, black tar and decked-out flowerbed, your heavy scent
not heaven sent not spent yet, just wandering around in the

air.

A good alphabet, be kind to it, be faithful, but one starts to get apathetic
when it
        does not respond,

like a dog who wanders off with the stick. Fuck you, dog, anyway.

                                Some poems on the table make me feel
sick.

At the playground, the playground, the playground: sweat and dirt and cookies.

      Your concerns are not my concerns, says one woman to another.

Must I "accede to its real presence

                which consists in its departure"? (Nancy)

Squirrel on the roof, ants in the sink, mouse in the pipe,
mold in the curtain, how cool the bellows.

87.

SOME FEARS

Arachnophobia, anthropophobia, barophobia, biblio (of spiders and of men, of gravity and books).

Catoptrophobia, dementophobia, ecophobia, eleuthero (of mirrors, insanity, of home, and freedom).

Epistemophobia (knowledge). Ergophobia (work). Felinophobia (cats). Gamophobia (marriage).

Genophobia, heliophobia, isolophobia, kopo (of sex, the sun, solitude, fatigue).

Logophobia (words). Melophobia (music). Metrophobia (poetry). Mnemophobia (memories).

Necrophobia, oneirophobia, ornithophobia, pedo (of death, dreams, birds, children).

Phasmophobia (ghosts). Somniphobia (sleep). Theophobia (God).
Tocophobia (pregnancy).

Uranophobia (Heaven). Xenophobia (strangers). Zoophobia (animals).

88.

NEW JERSEY

Whereas the cup is empty the back tight, the legs crossed.
Whereas this TV and the other TV and the other TV and the light:

        soft and white.

Whereas the bread: soft and white, the water in the pool, softened, whitened.

Whereas Nordic Track and Stephen King, Bush, Bush, and Grisham.
Of diet and of beer, of tile and of dog,

    of baby and of snack.

Soft and white breath of wire.

    Whereas the skin, the teeth, the nails, and the clothes:

softened, whitened

        Of softener and whitener. Of wire-breath.

89.

blue and steady

                                  fresh and red

        soft and white

                                        oh compass

90.

SOME COMPLICATIONS

A.

But the boy who murdered his parents and his sister had been beaten with a hose, tied to a tractor so he could not move.

Watered my garden. Two girls in the wading pool.

Asked the mother of son's friend if there were guns in the house.

Yes. But locked. OK. No problem!

B.

Vollmann reports that suicide rates drop dramatically in people older than forty. Because, as he rightly surmises, the absurdity of doing what nature will do anyway reveals itself. Of course, this passivity assumes that one is not in great pain, not anticipating causing great pain to others. And thus, if illness proves this second assumption false, I promise my husband blithely, I will destroy myself. I am aware of the complications such a promise can carry.

One wants the children to feel loved, and what I have seen is that the children of suicides (no matter the motive) do not feel loved.

Rather, worthless.

One I knew built a shrine to suicide in his closet. Did not feel loved.

Worthless.

91.

THE BEAUTIFUL

Outside, the wind is in the scrub oaks, the sun is in the grass. No longer
finding shelter in the cupboard of words I have made I lift my shirt and
reveal my wounds to the elements. Such drama is warranted by curiosity;
what really is at stake in these moments of exposure?

This too is a violence, though perhaps only to the self?

But nothing of the other goes away. Said one, we are at the end of our rope here, we are ready
to erase the circles we have drawn around ourselves:

Can we drink this water here? Should we breathe in that smell?

Momentous as a falling sun, a burned library, a diseased gut, a
wasp in the eaves is my baby's eye.

92.

MOTHER AND DAUGHTER 3

A.

"If mother love is, as some bioevolutionary and developmental psychologists as well as some cultural feminists believe, a 'natural,' or at least expectable, womanly script, what does it mean for women for whom scarcity and death have made that love frantic?" (Scheper-Hughes)

B.

The National Child Abuse and Neglect Data System (NCANDS) lists Colorado as third in the US for deaths from child abuse.

In 2006, 40,000 child abuse cases were investigated in Colorado. Of those, 8,700 were confirmed. In all, 24 children died of abuse and neglect.

Launced
"secure in

(*Research*: to go about seeking)

(Every researcher a predator)

safe and permanent families."

93.

Of men: Walked through the dark: jogger behind me: "overcoat of clay."
    (Dickinson)
Of gravity: And if I were to release my hold.
Of mirrors: The enigma of looking into one's own eyes as if the eyes of
    another: the "sudden appearance of the unavailable." (Nancy)
Of insanity: "The rhythmic range of words fills me with horror." (Roubaud)

94.

Of home: Majesty and Amber.
Of the sun: I cannot break into it, its daily resurrection, daily assault.

95.

Knowledge: I'm on a mission. I cannot stop.

Of work: The white plastic cup top, the cup in its sleeve, my hand on the cup-
sleeve, the weight of the full cup.

Of marriage: How are you feeling? What are you thinking? What are you reading?
What are you writing? Where are you going?

Sex: The inside of a tree is wet. This music is guided by God.

Of the sun: Where run to?

Of being alone: The inside of my lip is raw. Tastes raw.

Of fatigue: A bird taking flight over and over and over and over. A bird taking
flight over and over.

Of speaking: Run to the rock.

96.

Of music:

Of memories: Sidewalks and trees. Faces and rooms. My mother's voice: "Jula,"
her name for me, now in permanent disuse.

Of death: Cars at dawn cannot be counted.

97.

You cannot put

…

the light now
Prettier than

…

the slowest night

98.

Numbers: But why quantify? Each driver a reservoir of—

Dreams: His body behind mine. There is music and I hear it through *his* body, not through my own body.

Birds: Not like. Unlike. So very much uncaught.

Children: She was surprised and frightened when she noticed that I too was crying, that her sadness had made me cry.

Ghosts: Like ice that is and is not water.

Darkness: My breath that is and is not me.

99.

Sleep: Things among other things within a world closed upon itself.

God: "What is the grass?"

Animals: Tail of fox, nose of rabbit, haunch of weasel, neck of swan, tail of squirrel, spine of horse.

Pregnancy: Of which. That which. Within which. As. As if. If which. As that which is of. Of that which is within.

Words: Alice at six calls the baby "unavailable" says over and over, "Lucy, you're so unavailable!" By which she seems to mean

beloved.

100.

Is beloved "dear to the heart" more thought than said is dear precious noble or sore is sore like a stone is sore afflicted or inflamed is inflame to kindle to kindle wrath is wrath from wroth (maybe now we'll see) is wroth dear trashed dear aging is wroth from reid wound as the vine around the trunk the baby at my shin twined or wound is it pools and chairs is it blue and steady is twined mutual is mutual mutual is mutual from mutable as deception's from mutable is deception delusion beguilement or cunning is cunning cute like knowledge sharp is sharp like a joke or sharp like a slap like a blade or a cry is cry from citizen from hind or hand is to hand to offer to give back or return is turn to throw or rub or pierce or bore or strike is strike to delete to attack to deliver to sound like a bell is sound to speak to sing to utter to cry is this to cry is this is this

ACKNOWLEDGMENTS

American Poetry Review: "59. (The book about violence must be…)," "60. (Man goes constantly…)," "61. Colorado," "(The sun hurts)," "64. From General to Specific," "65. (I came to the conclusion…)

Bombay Gin: "1. (It won't snow again)," "2. (Salt's on the lands…)," "3. A Beginning," "5. (Hit my jaw)," "6. (Today was exhausting)," "7. (Sun on the windshield)," "8. (I pushed my face…)," "10. Fire," "11. Fire 2"

Calaveras: "35. *Consider This*," "41. (Lie down little girl…)," "42. *Two Narrative Poems*," "43. (Resting hands)," "44. (Cold and grand…)," "45. (A novelist calls me…," "46. *Dare Read.*"

Coconut: "75. (Up since three)," "77. (on the night of the day)," "81. Some More Research!," "82. (Enough of that)," "83. (*Whereas my mouth…*)"

Free Verse: "80. (It's about time to go…)"

Packington Review: "29. (About human dignity)," "32. (The useless mother's face)," "92. The Beautiful"

VOLT: "66. (Should I speak to you)," "67. Mother and Daughter 2," "68. (Here's a happy place)," "69. (A million billion fishes)"

Denver Quarterly: 12, 13, 24, 25, 26, 27, 38, 39

WORKS CITED

PRINT

Kathy Acker: *Empire of the Senseless: A Novel*
Guillaume Apollinaire: "April Night, 1915"
Georges Bataille: *Death and Sensuality: A Study of Eroticism and the Taboo*
Maurice Blanchot: *Lautréamont and Sade*
Margaret Wise Brown: *Four Fur Feet*
Emily Dickinson: *The Complete Poems*
Fyodor Dostoevsky: *Notes from Underground*
Donald G. Dutton: *The Psychology of Genocide, Massacres, and Extreme Violence: Why "Normal" People*
      Come to Commit Atrocities
Barbara Guest: *Rocks on a Platter*
Gerard Manley Hopkins: "Carrion Comfort"
Jean-Luc Nancy: *Noli Me Tangere: On the Raising of the Body*
Chuck Palahniuk: *Survivor: A Novel*
Michael Palmer*: Notes for Echo Lake*
Jacques Roubaud: *Some Thing Black*
John Ruskin: "The Pathetic Fallacy"
William Shakespeare: *Macbeth*
Nancy Scheper-Hughes: *Death Without Weeping: The Violence of Everyday Life in Brazil*
Michael Taussig: *Law in a Lawless Land: Diary of a Limpieza in Colombia*
William T. Vollmann: *Rising up and Rising Down: Some Thoughts on Violence, Freedom, and Urgent Means*
Walt Whitman: *Leaves of Grass*
C.D. Wright: *One Big Self: An Investigation*
Rhonda Zwillinger: *The Dispossessed Project*
The King James Bible
Webster's Dictionary

WEB

BBC News: http://news.bbc.co.uk/

Brady Campaign: http://www.bradycampaign.org/issues/gvstats/ kidsandguns/

5280: Denver's Magazine: http://www.5280.com/blog/?p=2239

The Department of Homeland Security: http://www.dhs.gov/index.shtm

Guns Accessories: http://www.gunaccessories.com/

Human Rights Watch: http://www.hrw.org/

Kempe Center for Prevention and Treatment of Child Abuse and Neglect:
	http://www.kempe.org/

The National Child Abuse and Neglect Data System: http://www.ndacan. cornell.edu

National Public Radio: www.npr.org

The New York Times: www.nyt.com

The Phobia List: http://phobialist.com/

WORKS CONSULTED

James Allen, ed.: *Without Sanctuary: Lynching Photography in America*

Hannah Arendt: *On Violence*

Walter Benjamin: "Critique of Violence"

Robert Capa: *Children of War, Children of Peace*

Israel W. Charny: *How Can we Commit the Unthinkable? Genocide: The Human Cancer*

Ernst Friedrich: *War against War!*

Jim Goldberg: *Raised by Wolves*

Ann Jones, Donna Ferrato: *Living with the Enemy*

Alessandra Mauro, ed.: *My Brother's Keeper: Documentary Photographers and Human Rights*

Mark Reinhardt, ed.: *Beautiful Suffering: Photography and the Traffic in Pain*

Roberto Saviano: *Gomorra: A Personal Journey into the Violent International Empire of Naples' Organized
	Crime System*

Elaine Scary: *The Body in Pain*

Susan Sontag: *Regarding the Pain of Others*

Elizabeth A. Stanko, ed.: *The Meanings of Violence*

Eric D. Weitz: *A Century of Genocide: Utopias of Race and Nation*

Tim Wride, James Ellroy, William J. Bratton: *Scene of the Crime: Photographs from the LAPD Archive*

Slavoj Žižek: *Violence*

Slavoj Žižek: *Welcome to the Desert of the Real*

Thank you to all who shared their stories with me and who granted permission for me to retell them here. Thank you to Steve Carr, Matthew Cooperman, Louise Elving, Brian Henry, Joseph Lease, Rusty Morrison, Jennifer Pap, John-Michael Rivera, Margaret Ronda, and Andrew Zawacki for reading and rich conversations. And thanks especially to Benjamin, Alice, and Lucy for giving me reasons to recoil not, and for sleeping in. Finally, thanks to Tim Roberts for collaborations and for love.

Julie Carr is the author of 12 books of poetry and prose, including *Climate*, co-written with Lisa Olstein (Essay Press 2022), *Real Life: An Installation* (Omindawn 2018), *Objects from a Borrowed Confession* (Ahsahta 2017), and *Someone Shot my Book* (University of Michigan Press 2018). Earlier books include *100 Notes on Violence* (Ahsahta 2010), *RAG* (Omnidawn, 2014), and *Think Tank* (Solid Objects 2015). With Jeffrey Robinson she is the co-editor of *Active Romanticism* (University of Alabama Press 2015). Her co-translation of Leslie Kaplan's *Excess-The Factory* was published by Commune Editions in 2018. *Mud, Blood, and Ghosts: Populism, Eugenics, and Spiritualism in the American West* was published by the University of Nebraska Press in 2023. *Underscore*, a book of poems, is forthcoming from Omnidawn in 2024.

Carr was a 2011-12 NEA fellow, is a Professor at the University of Colorado in Boulder in English and Creative Writing, and is chair of the Women and Gender Studies department. She has collaborated with dance artists K.J. Holmes and Gesel Mason. With Tim Roberts she is the co-founder of Counterpath Press, Counterpath Gallery, and Counterpath Community Garden in Denver. www.reallifeaninstallation.com; www.juliecarrpoet.com; www.counterpathpress.org

100 Notes on Violence

by Julie Carr

Cover art: "Red Hooded Figure" by Andres Serrano

Cover design by Jeffrey Pethybridge
Cover typeface: Avenir

Interior design by Laura Joakimson
Interior typeface: Apollo MT, and Eurostyle

Printed in the United States
by Books International,
Dulles, Virginia on Acid Free Archival Quality Recycled Paper

Publication of this book was made possible in part by gifts from Katherine & John Gravendyk
in honor of Hillary Gravendyk, Francesca Bell, Mary Mackey, and The New Place Fund

Omnidawn Publishing Oakland, California

Staff and Volunteers, Spring 2022

Rusty Morrison & Ken Keegan, senior editors & co-publishers
Laura Joakimson, production editor and poetry & fiction editor
Rob Hendricks, editor for Omniverse, poetry & fiction,
& post-pub marketing
Sharon Zetter, poetry editor & book designer
Jeffrey Kingman, copy editor
Liza Flum, poetry editor
Anthony Cody, poetry editor
Jason Bayani, poetry editor
Gail Aronson, fiction editor
Jennifer Metsker, marketing assistant
Jordyn MacKenzie, marketing assistant
Sophia Carr, marketing assistant